LIFE IN ANCIENT ROME

Joseph Farrell, Ph.D.

RUNNING PRESS
PHILADELPHIA · LONDON

Copyright © 1995 by Running Press
Printed in the United States. All rights reserved under the Pan-American and
International Copyright Conventions.

*This book may not be reproduced in whole or in part in any form or by any means, electronic
or mechanical, including photocopying, recording, or by any information storage and retrieval
system now known or hereafter invented, without written permission from the publisher.*

Canadian representatives: General Publishing Co., Ltd.,
30 Lesmill Road, Don Mills, Ontario M3B 2T6.

9 8 7 6 5 4 3 2 1
Digit on the right indicates the number of this printing.

Library of Congress Cataloging-in-Publication Number 94–67764

ISBN 1-56138-500-X

Cover design by Toby Schmidt
Book interior design by Christian Benton
Book interior illustrations by Michael S. Parker
Picture research by Susan Oyama
Edited by William King
The text was set in Berkeley and Castellar by Deborah Lugar.

Book cover and package interior illustrations: Scala/Art Resource, NY.
Package illustrations: Karl Kofoed.
Package back photograph: University of Pennsylvania Museum, Philadelphia
(Neg. # S4-141593)
Interior photos: Art Resource, NY: p. 17. Alinari/Art Resource, NY: pp. 5, 13, 16, 22, 28,
29, 39. Nimatallah/Art Resource, NY: p. 40. Scala/Art Resource, NY: pp. 31, 34. The
Library Company of Philadelphia: pp. 10–11, 23, 25, 32. Courtesy of the Library of
Congress Photoduplication Service: p. 63 (Neg. #LC-USA7-22082). University of
Pennsylvania Museum, Philadelphia: pp. 12 (Neg. #S4-95042), 14 (Neg. #S4-141594),
35 (Neg. #S8-73826). Photographs, pp. 18, 33: © Emmanuel M. Kramer.

This package may be ordered by mail from the publisher.
Please add $2.50 for postage and handling. *But try your bookstore first!*

Running Press Book Publishers
125 South Twenty-second Street
Philadelphia, Pennsylvania 19103–4399

A NOTE TO PARENTS:

This interactive, educational kit is designed to teach and entertain children, but it
contains small parts which could cause injury if swallowed. This kit should not be
used by children under four years of age without adult supervision. Please read the
complete instructions inside before using this kit.

—Running Press Book Publishers

CONTENTS

PART ONE:
Who Were the Romans?. 4
The Legend of Romulus and Remus
The Romans and Their City
A Timeline of Major Events
The Legend of Aeneas
Living in the City
The People of Rome
   Activity: Make Your Own Toga

PART TWO:
Make Your Own Roman Sundial. 36
   Activity: Counting in Latin
The Great Sundial of Augustus
Reconstruct a Replica of an Aquileian Sundial

PART THREE:
Living in Rome in 10 B.C.. 48
A Day in the Life
   Activity: Make a Roman Meal

PART FOUR:
The Romans and Their Influence Today 61
How Their Legacy Influences Our Lives

PART ONE:
WHO WERE THE ROMANS?

The Legend of Romulus and Remus

Many Latin cities were founded before Rome. One such city was Alba Longa, the "long white city." The king of Alba was Numitor, and he had a daughter, Rhea Silvia. Rhea was a Vestal Virgin, a priestess of the goddess Vesta, the Latin goddess of the hearth.

One night Rhea had a dream in which she saw the most handsome man she had ever beheld. He told her that she would become the mother of the greatest city on earth; and she asked, "How can this be, since I have promised Vesta never to marry and have children?" He replied, "All things are possible for the gods. And I who am with you am the mighty god of war, Mars, fearsome to man and god alike!"

With these words Rhea Silvia awoke, but she told no one about the dream. After nine months passed, she gave birth to twin boys. Her father thought she had broken her vow and was furious. As punishment, he had her buried alive, and had the twins placed in a basket, which was set afloat in the Tiber River.

The twins floated to a place on the bank of the river, where they probably would have died. But as luck would have it, a mother wolf happened by and noticed them.

PART ONE: WHO WERE THE ROMANS?

Romulus, Remus, and the she-wolf have become a famous symbol for the city of Rome.

And instead of harming them in any way, the she-wolf nursed them and raised them as if they were her own cubs.

In this way the twins, who were named Romulus and Remus, grew to be strong young men. Eventually they returned to Alba Longa and avenged their mother's death. With a band of volunteers from Alba Longa and the surrounding towns, Romulus and Remus founded a new city overlooking the place on the Tiber where their basket had come ashore. But when the time came to decide who would rule the city, they fell to arguing, then fighting, and before he realized it, Romulus had killed his twin brother. Romulus became the first king of Rome, left to rule alone.

The Romans and Their City

The Romans lived in a city, Rome, near the west coast of Italy on the banks of the Tiber River. In very ancient times, Italy was the home of many different peoples from other places, including Etruscans, Gauls, Sabellians, Greeks, and the Latins, the group to which the Romans belonged. Each of these peoples spoke a different language and had different customs. Some, like the Latins and Etruscans, lived mainly in cities. Others, like the Sabellians and the Gauls, lived in nomadic communities with tribal governments. While all of these peoples influenced one

This gathering of Romans, depicting from left to right, a German, an Egyptian, a Scot, a Jew, a Phrygian, and a Greek, shows the diverse range of ethnic groups that lived in Rome.

another, they all also held on to their own traditions long after they came to know the ways of other cultures.

The Romans were a Latin people. Latium, the land of the Latins, is very close to the middle of Italy. Rome, one of the youngest Latin cities, was in the northernmost part of Latium. It was a small town, just an outpost in those early years, but because it was built away from the coast, it was safe from pirate raids. And its position on the Tiber gave it access to the sea and to some neighboring salt mines. The people who lived farther inland needed salt both for themselves and for the animals they raised. So the Romans were in a good position to do business with the other peoples of Italy, and their city grew steadily.

By trading, the Romans got to know the customs of their neighbors in Italy, and because Rome was a good place to do business, many foreigners moved into Rome from other towns. But ancient Italy was not a peaceful place. Neighboring peoples, seeing the advantages that Rome possessed, wanted to control it themselves. In fact, tradition tells us that most of the kings who ruled in Rome during its earliest period were not Romans, but either Sabellians or Etruscans. During this time many families from other Italian peoples settled in Rome and added their customs to those that the Romans had inherited from their Latin ancestors.

In about 500 B.C. the Romans expelled the Etruscan kings who then had control of their city. Rome then became a republic, a government of officials elected by the citizens. Decisions were made by the senate, an elected council made up mostly of men who had formerly held office in the government. Under this government (which lasted for about 500 years!), Roman influence spread throughout Italy and the entire known world.

At its height in the 2nd century, the Roman Empire covered much of Europe, as well as parts of Africa and Asia. Many different peoples lived within this vast area, and each contributed to the civilization of Rome. Colonies were founded by the Romans as their population grew—cities like Florentia (modern Florence, Italy), Corduba (Cordova, Spain), Colonia Agrippensis (Cologne, Germany), and Eburacum (York, England). Other peoples, like the Gauls and the Egyptians, became friends or allies of the Roman people as a result of peaceful contacts or through wars. Many of these cities, like Athens and Corinth in Greece, were much older than Rome and had their own customs and forms of government, most of which they kept.

In this way, the Romans gradually came to control a very large empire that included many different peoples. But the Roman Empire was not a country divided into smaller parts like the United States. Instead, it was a huge number of individual relationships between the people of Rome and those who lived in the other cities and towns of the Mediterranean world. Some of the people who lived in these other cities became citizens of Rome as well; but for a long time this was a very special privilege. Most people had the status of allies or subjects, and so had fewer rights and privileges than Roman citizens.

PART ONE: WHO WERE THE ROMANS?

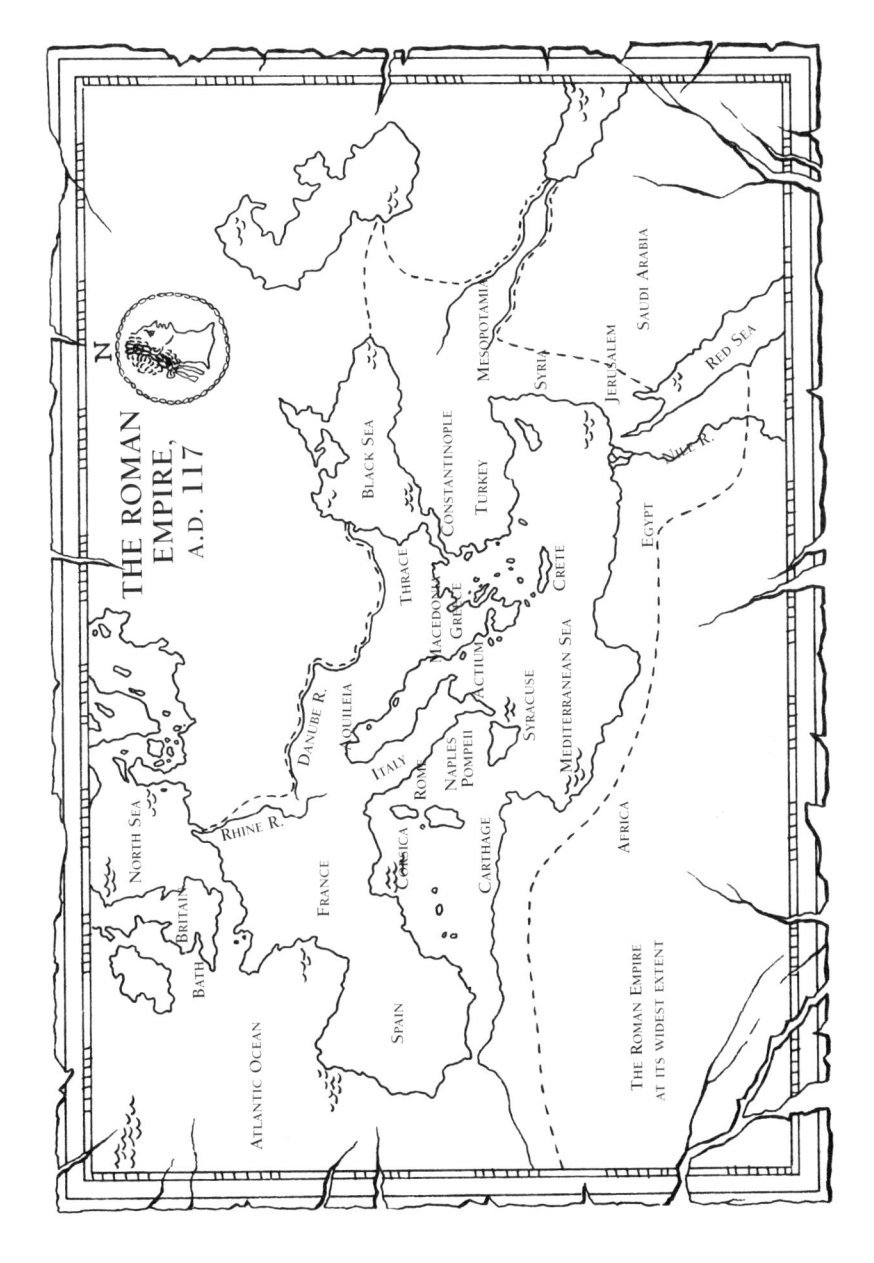

A Timeline of Major Events

1100 B.C.: Trojan War. Voyage of Aeneas from Troy to Italy.

753–509 B.C.: Regal Period. Rome is ruled by a series of seven kings; the first is Romulus.

509–281 B.C.: Early Republican Period. Roman influence spreads throughout the Italian peninsula.

281–146 B.C.: Middle Republican Period. Roman influence spreads throughout the Mediterranean.

> 264–241 B.C.: First Punic War. Rome defeats Carthage, a Phoenician city on the north African coast.
>
> 218–201 B.C.: Second Punic War. The great Carthaginian general Hannibal is defeated by the Roman general Scipio.
>
> 149–146 B.C.: Third Punic War. Scipio's adopted son, P. Cornelius Scipio Aemilianus, destroys Carthage.

146–29 B.C.: Late Republican Period. The strain of running a world empire creates problems in Roman government and society. Three civil wars are fought for control of government.

29 B.C.–180 A.D.: Early Imperial Period. The Romans govern their empire in peace and spread their culture throughout the western provinces.

> 14–68 A.D.: Julio-Claudian Emperors (Augustus, Tiberius, Caligula, Claudius, Nero).

69 A.D.: After Nero is assassinated, a civil war is fought over control of the empire.

69–96 A.D.: Flavian Dynasty (Vespasian, Titus, Domitian). Vespasian restores peace and is succeeded as emperor by his sons.

96–180 A.D.: The Five Good Emperors (Nerva, Trajan, Hadrian, Antoninus Pius, Marcus Aurelius). This is the longest period of peace in Roman history.

180–284 A.D.: Middle Imperial Period. Few emperors can hold on to power for long.

285–565 A.D.: Late Imperial Period. Major changes in the empire leading finally to its disintegration and to the creation of the new world of the Middle Ages.

284–305 A.D.: Diocletian divides the empire into eastern and western parts, each ruled by its own emperor. Later emperors try to reunite the empire, but cannot hold it together because of internal problems and war.

324–337 A.D.: Constantine makes Christianity the official religion of the empire, and moves the emperor's residence to the eastern city of Byzantium, which he renames Constantinople.

410 A.D.: Sack of Rome by an army of Visigoths under the command of Alaric.

475–476 A.D.: Romulus Augustulus, last emperor of the western empire.

527–565 A.D.: Justinian briefly unifies the empire for the last time.

All during this time the Roman government remained basically the same as it had been in 500 B.C., when Rome was a small, unimportant city with no empire to govern. But after the Romans gained control of so much territory and became responsible for governing so many different peoples, their republican form of government did not work as well. By the end of the first century B.C., it became clear that the empire could be run more efficiently with one man at the top.

The problem was how to choose this man, and a series of civil wars was fought before one man established himself as the right one to run the empire. This man was Caesar Augustus, who kept most of the traditional forms of government but reorganized them into a new system that was capable of running a worldwide empire. The system he put in place changed and developed over time, but the imperial government lasted for centuries and its effects can still be felt today.

By the first century A.D., Rome was one of the largest cities in the world, home to a million people or more. It had become the center of government for all the peoples who lived around the Mediterranean Sea, many of whom—Greeks, Egyptians, Syrians, Jews, Gauls, Libyans, and others—had come to live in Rome. The Romans themselves loved to think about how

Roman coins depicted political leaders, much like our currency does today. This one features the emperor Augustus.

PART ONE: WHO WERE THE ROMANS?

This famous statue of Augustus, "Augustus of Prima Porta," now resides in the Vatican Museum.

The ruins of the courtyard of a wealthy Roman home

much the city had changed. On the top of the Palatine Hill, where many of the most important Romans lived in houses that were like palaces, they kept a very old, small hut which they believed was the home of their first king, Romulus. The contrast between this ancient cottage and the beautiful marble buildings around it clearly showed how far the Romans had come.

PART ONE: WHO WERE THE ROMANS?

The Legend of Aeneas

As we've seen, traditional Romans respected their ancestors and their national customs more than anything else. This is particularly true with the story of Aeneas.

The Romans believed that their first ancestors came to Italy from Troy. After the Greeks destroyed the city of the Trojans, who lived at the eastern end of the Mediterranean Sea, a few Trojan survivors joined forces and sailed west to found new cities. One of these Trojan survivors was Aeneas, son of Venus, the goddess of love, and the hero Anchises. He fought alongside his cousin Hector against Achilles, Ulysses, and the rest of the Greeks in the Trojan War, which lasted ten years. The Greeks were unable to conquer the Trojans by force; but when they pretended to give up the war and sail home, they left behind a gigantic wooden horse inside which they hid their best soldiers. The Trojans, thinking that the Greeks had left for good, brought the horse inside their city walls and celebrated their victory. That night, while the Trojans were sleeping, the Greek soldiers climbed out of the horse, set the city on fire, and began to kill all the Trojans.

At this point Aeneas, who was sleeping, was warned in a dream to wake up, gather his family, friends, and household gods, and sail to Italy. There he and his descendants were to rule over a new kingdom.

Aeneas obeyed this dream, which came from the gods. His father Anchises was old and lame, and his son Ascanius was very small. So Aeneas had to carry Anchises on his shoulders while he held the hand of Ascanius, who had to run alongside to keep up with him. After many adventures they made it to Italy, where Aeneas, Ascanius, and their descendants founded many cities in a district called Latium. The people who lived in these cities were called Latins and the language they spoke, too, was Latin.

This sculpture, probably created by the great 17th-century sculptor Giovanni Bernini, depicts Aeneas as he flees from the Greeks.

In later times, many Romans claimed that they were descended from one of the Trojan families that settled the cities of Latium. One family in particular claimed that their ancestor, Ascanius, had changed his name to Iulus [ee-YOO-loos]. This was the Julian clan. Their best known member was the famous general and politician, Gaius Iulius Caesar [Latin: GA-ee-oos YOO-lee-oos KYE-sar; English: GUY-us JOO-lee-us SEE-zer].

PART ONE: WHO WERE THE ROMANS?

The Pont du Gard aqueduct in Nimes, France

Living in the City

Ancient Rome was a lot like modern New York City, Tokyo, or Mexico City. There were paved streets, large public buildings and monuments, libraries and picture galleries, parks, and grand private homes for the wealthy. There were even apartment buildings, called *insulae* [IN-soo-lye], or "islands," for other people.

One of the most impressive things about the city was its water system. Roman engineers built long channels called *aqueducts* from the tops of mountains dozens of miles away that led into the city. In this way they were able to bring abundant supplies of pure, fresh water into every neighborhood and even into some private homes. They also built an extensive system of sewers, something that no other city had until many centuries later. Without these engineering feats, a city the size of Rome would have been unlivably filthy and full of disease.

The city was divided into thirty regions and many more neighborhoods, each with its own name, a water fountain, and a public shrine. Each of the different sections of the city had its own character. The eighth region held the Forum, the ancient center of the city, which contained the senate house, the law courts, some of the oldest and most magnificent temples in the city, the mint (where money was coined), and other businesses. In the ninth region, along the banks of the Tiber, was the home of, among others, the Jewish community of Rome. The tenth region was nearby and contained the Palatine Hill. Here were found many

The ruins of the Roman Forum as it appears today

of the most fashionable homes, including that of the emperor Augustus.

Unlike modern cities, Rome for a long time had no police force or public fire department. By the end of the republic Rome could be a very dangerous place. Several people kept private armies which they used to both protect themselves and terrify enemies. The emperors put an end to this practice, and used the army of the state, which they controlled, as a public police force when necessary. Fire brigades were maintained by landlords and real estate speculators, who would appear at burning buildings with their firemen. The firemen would then stand by while their employer offered the owner of the burning building some money for their property. If the owner refused, the buyer would let the building burn and offer less money as more of the building was destroyed. When the owner finally gave in, the buyer would order his brigade into action, saving whatever was left of his purchase!

The People of Rome

Rome contained people from all over the world. Some people came to Rome and adopted Roman customs, but others held on to their traditional ways. If you walked the streets of ancient Rome, you would have seen all sorts of people.

The Traditional Roman Aristocracy

As the city grew, the number of people who came from old Roman families became small compared with the number of immigrants. But because the older families controlled most of the city's wealth and power, they are the ones we know the most about.

The men of the most important families were usually members of the senate. Their ancestors had been important statesmen and generals down through the centuries. The most respected career for a Roman gentleman involved running for a *magistracy*, or political office. If he was successful, he would eventually earn the right to join the senate himself, where he and other former magistrates would discuss matters of state and recommend what the empire should do. At some point in his career he would serve as an officer in the army and on a staff that was sent to govern one of the provinces. Roman aristocrats prized these appointments because they added to their personal distinction and to that of their family. And just as private citizens tried to befriend members of the great senatorial families to protect their interests, the people of a foreign city or province might ask a senator who had once been their governor to appeal to the emperor on their behalf. If his appeal was successful, the province might erect a statue or some other monument in his honor.

Some men from wealthy and powerful families did not enter politics. There might be several reasons for this. For one thing, senators were not allowed to take part in certain forms of business. Owning a farm or estate was considered the best occupation for a senator. Trading companies, tax collecting, and other businesses were considered either too risky or too undignified for a senator.

But many men, some of them brothers of senators, went into these businesses and became extremely wealthy. Others inherited enough money to live without working and spent their time traveling, reading and writing, collecting art, and enjoying themselves. Still others may have been born without a great deal of money, but became very successful businessmen. All of these people were called "knights" or "equestrians" [*equites,* EH-kwee-tays] because, in earlier times, they were thought to be wealthy enough to own a horse to ride into battle. During the empire many knights helped the emperor govern some parts of the empire, and some knights enjoyed careers just as distinguished as those of most senators.

The women of the upper classes had very few opportunities for careers. But their lives could be interesting just the same. Unlike many ancient societies, the Romans allowed women to own property and conduct business on their own, and

The dress of a typical upper-class Roman couple

many women were excellent businesspeople. The wives, sisters, and daughters of senators were often very influential in politics as well. Although they couldn't sit in the senate or vote, they often played an important role in political discussions involving the men to whom they were related. They were also in charge of matchmaking between the younger members of their families. This was an important job. If a young man and woman from two powerful families married, it might be the beginning of an important political alliance. And if an ambitious young man were allowed to marry a distinguished senator's daughter, it could be very helpful to the young man's career.

Besides these roles, upper-class women were in a position to help both the men and women of the lower classes. Women were mainly responsible for running their households. In a wealthy family, this might be a large job. Many upper-class Romans had several residences throughout Italy, each of which would be staffed with servants, most of them slaves. Managing all these people

Although her name is forgotten, we do know that this Roman woman must have been well-to-do.

must have been a full-time occupation. In addition, a slave who was well liked and had given good service might win his or her freedom. It would only be natural for a former owner, man or woman, to take an interest in promoting the freedman's future career, perhaps with a loan or references. A woman who ran a large household might play a very important role in helping her former servants to prosper and to rise through the ranks of society.

The Common People

The Roman aristocracy was very small. By the time the population of the city reached one million, only about four hundred men were members of the senate. There were more knights, but the number was still small compared to the total population. Most of the people who lived in Rome were from families who came from outside Rome. Some

In the marketplace, servants might draw water for their master while he sold his wares.

came of their own choice. Others were slaves, prisoners from wars the Romans won. Many in Rome had been slaves themselves or had ancestors who were slaves, but it was fairly easy for a slave to become a *freedman* [*libertus*, lee-BEAR-toos], either by earning freedom through service to a kind master or else by saving up enough money to buy it. A freedman's status was better than a slave's, though not as high as that of a person who was born in freedom. But his or her children would at least enjoy free birth along with the full rights of Roman citizenship. Some foreigners even sold themselves into slavery, hoping by hard work to win their freedom and become citizens themselves.

Social relations

The Romans were very concerned with social status, and many of their customs reflected this concern. When they went to the theater, for instance, they sat in sections determined by their rank: senators in one place, knights in another, and so on. They even entered the theater through different doorways, depending on their rank.

People of higher orders dressed in more ornate clothing than those in lower ranks as a way of signaling their status. But even though the social ranks were carefully distinguished, members of the different orders depended on one another. For instance, a Roman gentleman hardly ever appeared in public alone. Normally he was accompanied by a crowd of people whom he called "friends" [*amici*, ah-MEE-kee]. But these friends were not just people whose company he enjoyed. He was their "patron," a kind of sponsor or protector. They were his "clients" [*clientes*, or

PART ONE: WHO WERE THE ROMANS?

The Roman's attention to social status even extended to their architecture. In theatres like the Colosseum, for instance, the columns indicated the status of those within. The bottom column is very plain and is known as the Doric order. Doric columns indicated where the poorer citizens would enter. The middle column is of the more elaborate Ionic order. The top column is the Corinthian order. The more elaborate the doorway, the wealthier the theatergoer.

leaners]. Most of them were people less wealthy and powerful than himself who depended on him to use his wealth and position to protect their interests. If they were in legal trouble, he might act as their lawyer, or find someone who would. If they needed money, he might lend it to them. If they needed advice, they would turn to him. In return for such services, these friends could be counted on for other sorts of favors. A humble friend could vote for his patron if he stood for election. A more frequent favor was to accompany his patron in public so other people would realize how important and popular his patron was.

Dress and Style

Aristocratic Romans were very conspicuous in the street. For one thing, there was the crowd of "friends" that followed them everywhere. They also wore the traditional Roman costume, the *toga*, which was a heavy woolen garment that had to be wrapped around the body with great care. (Romans never wore pants. In fact, when Roman travellers first learned of foreign peoples whose men did wear pants, they thought that such dress made these men look like women!) Senators wore a broad purple stripe on the borders of their togas. They also wore a special sort of shoe. Knights wore a toga with a narrow stripe, and on their hands were golden rings. Freedmen often had to wear a special sort of cap declaring their status. The Romans took these customs very seriously, and passed laws forbidding people to wear the dress of any class but their own.

PART ONE: WHO WERE THE ROMANS?

Activity: Make Your Own Toga

THE TOGA WAS THE OFFICIAL ROMAN NATIONAL GARMENT AND WAS ONLY WORN BY ROMANS. THE POET VERGIL DESCRIBED THE ROMANS AS "THE RACE THAT WEARS THE TOGA." THIS WAS SAID TO BE THE EMPEROR AUGUSTUS'S FAVORITE LINE IN ALL OF VERGIL'S POETRY. WITH A FEW OBJECTS FROM AROUND THE HOUSE, YOU CAN DRESS LIKE A ROMAN TOO!

FIRST, FIND A LONG TEE-SHIRT THAT ALMOST REACHES DOWN TO YOUR KNEES. THIS WOULD BE SIMILAR TO THE TUNIC THAT A ROMAN WOULD WEAR UNDERNEATH THEIR TOGA. A REAL TOGA WOULD BE A LARGE PIECE OF WOOL MEASURING ABOUT TEN FEET ON EACH SIDE. YOU CAN IMITATE THIS BY USING A LARGE, SQUARE BEDSHEET.

HANG THE SHEET ON YOUR LEFT ARM. DRAPE THE SHEET AROUND YOUR BACK, UNDER YOUR RIGHT ARM, ACROSS YOUR CHEST, AND THEN OVER YOUR LEFT SHOULDER. TIE THE ENDS TOGETHER IN A TIGHT KNOT.

MAKE SURE THAT YOU LEAVE A BIG FOLD ACROSS YOUR CHEST. THIS FOLD WAS CALLED THE *SINUS* [SEE-NOOS], AND THE ROMANS USED IT AS A POCKET. PUT ON A PAIR OF SANDALS AND YOU'RE READY FOR A VISIT TO THE COLOSSEUM!

LIFE IN ANCIENT ROME

This statue displays an excellent example of the traditional Roman garment, the toga.

Roman women wore dresses of various kinds, depending on the occasion. In public, married ladies and all women of the upper classes were supposed to wear a long gown called a *stola*. Most women were fond of wearing jewelry, similar to what women wear today, but often much more (if they could afford it). Many women also liked to have their hair done in very elaborate ways. Wealthy ladies might even keep a professional hairstylist on their household staff! Just like today, styles changed over time, as we can see from the statues of great Roman ladies that have been found.

Roman women were very fashion conscious and wore their hair in elaborate styles.

The common people dressed much less formally than the senators and the knights. Most men simply wore *tunics*, a kind of long shirt tied at the waist. Women could wear a wide variety of dresses. Many people kept the traditional clothing of their native country. Others might dress according to the custom of their religion. For example, during the empire, many in Rome worshipped the Egyptian goddess Isis. A worshipper of Isis might shave their head completely bald and wear a bright orange-yellow gown.

Of course, some Romans dressed to express their own taste and personality, but they also dressed, much more than we do, to tell other people about their place in society. If you saw a man in a dirty toga, it didn't mean he was too lazy to wash it. Instead, he might be wearing it for a special reason. It might be that he was a defendant in a court of law, or that someone in his family had died. Both of these occasions called for the wearing of a toga that was gray and dingy. By the same token, a man in a brilliant white toga wasn't just neat. He was probably running for office, which required that he wear a toga that had been whitened. People would call him a *candidatus* [can-dee-DAH-toos, "whitened man"].

Lifestyle

Members of the aristocracy, the senators and knights, led lives of great privilege. They often owned grand homes in the most fashionable districts of the city. They might have extensive collections of art, enormous libraries, private pleasure gardens, and a *familia*, or staff of slaves, numbering

PART ONE: WHO WERE THE ROMANS?

Worshippers offer a sacrifice to the goddess Isis.

Many villas of wealthy Romans contained open courtyards.

in the hundreds to keep everything running. The familia might include doctors, astrologers, and tutors for the children, in addition to butlers, cooks, and other household staff.

A more humble family could not afford such luxuries, but there were some entertainments enjoyed by rich and poor alike. The Colosseum hosted exhibitions of gladiators.

PART ONE: WHO WERE THE ROMANS?

The sand floor of the Colosseum concealed the labyrinth of passages and chambers (shown here) where animals were kept.

Shows like this were popular with everyone. So were chariot races, animal exhibitions, plays, and other kinds of shows.

Chariot races were a special favorite. In these events, highly trained drivers would guide their teams around a long, narrow course in one of their great "circuses" or race tracks like the Circus Maximus or the Circus of Domitian.

It was a dangerous event because the horses picked up a tremendous amount of speed on the long straight-aways, and then had to make a sharp turn before heading back to the finish line. There were often accidents at this turning post, as many drivers tried to turn as quickly and tightly as possible.

The drivers were organized into different teams like the Blues and the Greens, and each of the teams had loyal fans who cheered them and wore their colors. While most of the drivers were slaves, some of them were as popular as many of today's sports stars.

Chariot races were very popular in ancient Rome.

A modern reproduction of an ancient Roman helmet worn by a gladiator

Rich and poor alike used the public baths. Rather than bathing at home, most Romans went after the business day to bathe in special buildings constructed just for that purpose. Some of these, like the Baths of Agrippa or the Baths of Caracalla, were huge public buildings with beautiful architecture and decorations. The water was heated to different temperatures by wood-burning furnaces under the floor. Some baths had picture galleries, restaurants, and other services within them or nearby. They could accommodate many bathers at once, and so became great places to meet people, talk, read, relax, have lunch, and escape from the round of daily cares.

PART TWO:
MAKE YOUR OWN ROMAN SUNDIAL

The Roman day, like ours, was based on the sun. But the way they told time was different.

Just as we do, the Romans called the time when the sun was up the "day," or, in Latin, *dies* [DEE-ace], and the time when it was down the "night," or *nux* [NOOKS]. The day and the night together lasted twenty-four hours in all, just as they do now; but here is where things become different. Each of the twenty-four hours in our day and night is exactly the same length as all the others—sixty minutes, no more, no less. In the summer the day can last as long as fifteen modern hours, and the night only nine. In the winter, the day gets as short as nine hours, while it is the night that lasts longer. But the Romans divided their day and night into exactly twelve hours, or *horae* [HOE-rye], each, no matter what time of year it was. This means that their hours were hardly ever sixty minutes long. In the summer, when the sun was up from about 5:30 A.M. to 8:30 P.M. our time, a *hora* of daylight would last about 48 minutes, and a *hora* of night about 72 minutes. But in the winter, when the sun rose at 7:00 A.M. and set at 5:00 P.M., it was just the opposite.

PART TWO: MAKE YOUR OWN ROMAN SUNDIAL

Activity: Counting in Latin

1	I	one	unus/una/unum [OO-NUS / OO-NAH / OO-NUM]
2	II	two	duo [DOO-OH]
3	III	three	tres/tres/tria [TRACE / TREE-AH]
4	IV	four	quattuor [KWAH-TOO-OR]
5	V	five	quinque [KWEEN-KWEH]
6	VI	six	sex [SEX]
7	VII	seven	septem [SEP-TEM]
8	VIII	eight	octo [AWK-TOH]
9	IX	nine	nouem [NOH-WEM]
10	X	ten	decem [DEH-KEM]
11	XI	eleven	undecim [OON-DECKIM]
12	XII	twelve	duodecim [DOO-OD-DECKIM]

Some Latin words change their ending depending on whether they refer to a boy or man, a girl or woman, or a thing. To mean "one boy" the Romans would say "puer unus" [POO-air OO-nus], but "one girl" would be "puella una" [poo-ELL-ah OO-nah] and "one rock" would be "saxum unum" [SACK-sum OO-num]; "three boys" or "three girls" would be "pueri" or "puellae tres" [POO-airee or poo-ELL-i TRACE] and "three rocks" would be "saxa tria" [SACK-sah TREE-ah]. The numbers 2, 4, 5, 6, 7, 8, 9, and 10 do not change in this way.

You can see where the Romans got their numerals by counting on your fingers. "Unus" (= I) is one finger. "Duo" (= II) is two fingers. "Quinque" (= V) is the shape that your hand makes when you open all five fingers. "Decem" (= X) is the shape of two open hands with fingers spread, one under the other, the lower one upside-down. "Quattuor" (= IV) is "one before five" and "sex" (= VI) is one after five. Can you figure out the rest?

The Great Sundial of Augustus in the Campus Martius

The first emperor of Rome, Caesar Augustus, devoted a lot of time and money to beautifying the city. He liked to boast that he found the city built of brick and left it built of marble. In his day the northwest part of the city, the Campus Martius, had lots of open space, and it

Part Two: Make Your Own Roman Sundial

was here that, in 10 B.C., he built a great plaza in honor of his achievements.

The plaza contained an enormous sundial. In fact, it would be better to say that the plaza *was* a sundial. On its pavement, which covered thousands of square feet, were inscribed the hours of the day and the seasons of the year. In the middle was an obelisk, 90 feet high, that Augustus had brought to Rome after his victory in a war against the Egyptians. An Egyptian ruler had the obelisk made as an offering to the god of the sun but Augustus used it as the pointer for his colossal sundial.

A large obelisk, like this one in the Plaza Montecitorio, was used to tell time in the Campus Martius.

The Ara Pacis Augustae

There were two other monuments near the sundial. One was the Ara Pacis Augustae [AH-ra PAH-kis ow-GOOS-tie, "altar of the Augustan peace"], dedicated by the senate in 9 B.C. in honor of the peaceful conditions established throughout the empire under Augustus's leadership. The altar was placed so that on Augustus's birthday, at the hour of his birth, the shadow of the pointer fell in the direction of the altar. The other monument nearby was the tomb of Augustus, which he himself began to have built some twenty years earlier. The message here seems to be that time will someday run out for everyone, even for the most powerful man on earth.

The Roman Calendar

Just as our days and hours are a little like Roman ones, so, too, are our months and years. But just as before, there are important differences.

All of our months have Roman names, and some of these come from the Roman numbers you already know. In the name "September" you can see and hear the number "septem" (seven), and so on for October, November, and December. In addition, the early Romans called July "Quintilis" and August "Sextilis," which mean "Fifth Month" and "Sixth Month." The names were changed in honor of the first two Caesars, Julius and Augustus. (The senate offered to change the name of another month to honor the third Caesar, Tiberius; but they decided against it when he asked them what they were planning to do to honor the thirteenth Caesar!)

There is a problem here, though. December, which means "Tenth Month," is really the twelfth month of the year, as we know it was in Roman times as well. But we also know that when the Romans elected consuls, who were the top officials of their government, they entered office on March 1. (This is why, until 1937, the President of the

United States also entered office on March 1st.) So March must have once been the first month of their year, before the Romans began writing about their own history.

Reconstruct a Replica of an Aquileian Sundial

Inside the slab of rock that came with this kit is a replica of an ancient sundial like those found in Aquileia, Italy. All of the sundials that were used in Rome, like the one built by Augustus and described on page 38, were made to sit on a specific site. The sundial that you'll construct, though, has been adapted so that it will work in most parts of North America. If you live in the extreme northern or southern parts of the continent, though, you'll probably want to adjust the gnomon for your area.

In this kit you should have:
* a rectangular slab of rock that contains the pieces of the sundial
* a cardboard gnomon
* a wooden excavation tool

To reconstruct the sundial you'll also need:
* some newspaper or a plastic bag to cover your work surface
* a bucket or container of water

Part Two: Make Your Own Roman Sundial

* a soft brush; old toothbrushes or paintbrushes are best
* paper towels
* white glue; Elmer's Glue-All works well
* brown shoe polish (optional)

It's now time to reconstruct the sundial! The first thing you'll need to do is to carefully remove the pieces of the sundial from the clay. Take your time doing this—allow yourself at least an hour, as this can be very messy if you're not careful. You'll want to work outdoors or indoors on an easy-to-clean surface. Cover your workspace with newspaper or the plastic bag.

1) Place the slab of rock in the bucket of water. Let it soak for at least five minutes. Remove the slab and pat it dry with the towels. Don't throw away the water.

2) Using the wooden spatula, dig out the pieces of the sundial by carefully scraping away the loose clay. If you are having trouble removing the clay, soak the block some more.

Be careful while handling the pieces of the sundial, as some of the pieces might be sharp! Work slowly and try not to damage or break any of the pieces. Don't worry if you do though—you'll be able to glue them together later.

3) Clean the pieces of clay by rinsing them in the water while using the soft brush to remove any excess clay. Be sure to clean the edges well, as they must be dirt-free for the glue to work properly. When all of the pieces are clean, pour out the leftover clay and water into a disposable container; do not pour it down the drain.

Pat the clay pieces with the towels and let them sit out overnight on a piece of newspaper. If you want to speed up the drying process, use a hair dryer.

4) After the pieces have dried, try to find the ones that fit together. Once you've found two pieces that fit together, apply the glue and hold the pieces together for at least 30 seconds. Don't worry if you use too much glue since you'll be able to scrape off the extra glue later. Press the pieces together firmly, but not too hard. Carefully set the glued pieces aside to dry. Wait as long as the instructions on the glue tell you to wait. It's usually between 30 minutes and an hour.

5) Next, find two more pieces and glue them together. With a little time and patience, you'll soon have reconstructed your sundial! After it's completely assembled, scrape off any extra glue.

PART TWO: MAKE YOUR OWN ROMAN SUNDIAL

6) Now you're ready to set up the dial! First, slide the short side of the gnomon between the two notches in the center of the sundial. The pointed end should face towards the XII.

7) Place the sundial on a flat surface where sunlight shines throughout the day. Examine the sundial right before noon. The shadow of the gnomon should fall on the XII marker. If it doesn't, rotate the sundial until it does. Remember, though, to include the adjustment from the chart on page 47. For instance, if you are setting up your sundial on April 1st, the shadow should line up with the XII at 12:05 clock time. If you don't use the chart on page 47, your sundial time will always be slightly incorrect!

8) Once you start keeping time with your sundial, you'll need to take the difference between "solar" time and "mean time" into account. "Mean time" is the time that our clocks are based upon. In mean time, 60 minutes always make up an hour and 24 hours always make up a day. The sundial utilizes "solar time." Since the Earth doesn't travel in a precise circle around the sun, a solar day might only be 23 hours and 50 minutes long or 24 hours and 10 minutes long, instead of exactly 24 hours long. The chart on page 47 tells you how many minutes to add or subtract to the sundial time to tell the correct mean time.

9) Optional: You may want to coat the sundial with brown shoe polish to make it look nicer. Once the dial is positioned properly, you can also glue the gnomon to the sundial to make sure the gnomon does not become dislodged. When you do this though, make sure you correctly put the gnomon in the slot.

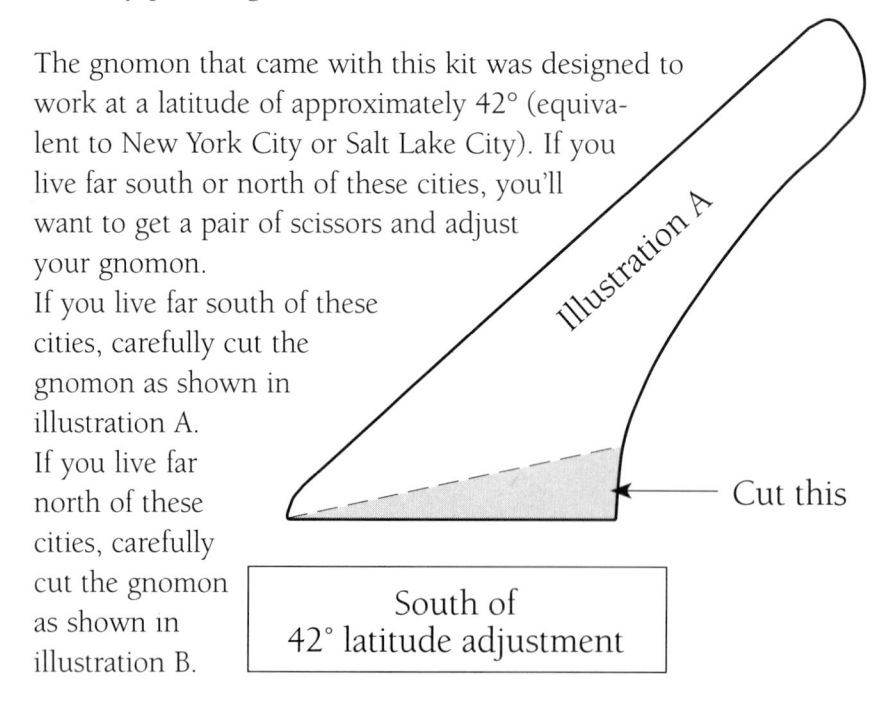

The gnomon that came with this kit was designed to work at a latitude of approximately 42° (equivalent to New York City or Salt Lake City). If you live far south or north of these cities, you'll want to get a pair of scissors and adjust your gnomon.
If you live far south of these cities, carefully cut the gnomon as shown in illustration A.
If you live far north of these cities, carefully cut the gnomon as shown in illustration B.

Illustration A

Cut this

South of 42° latitude adjustment

PART TWO: MAKE YOUR OWN ROMAN SUNDIAL

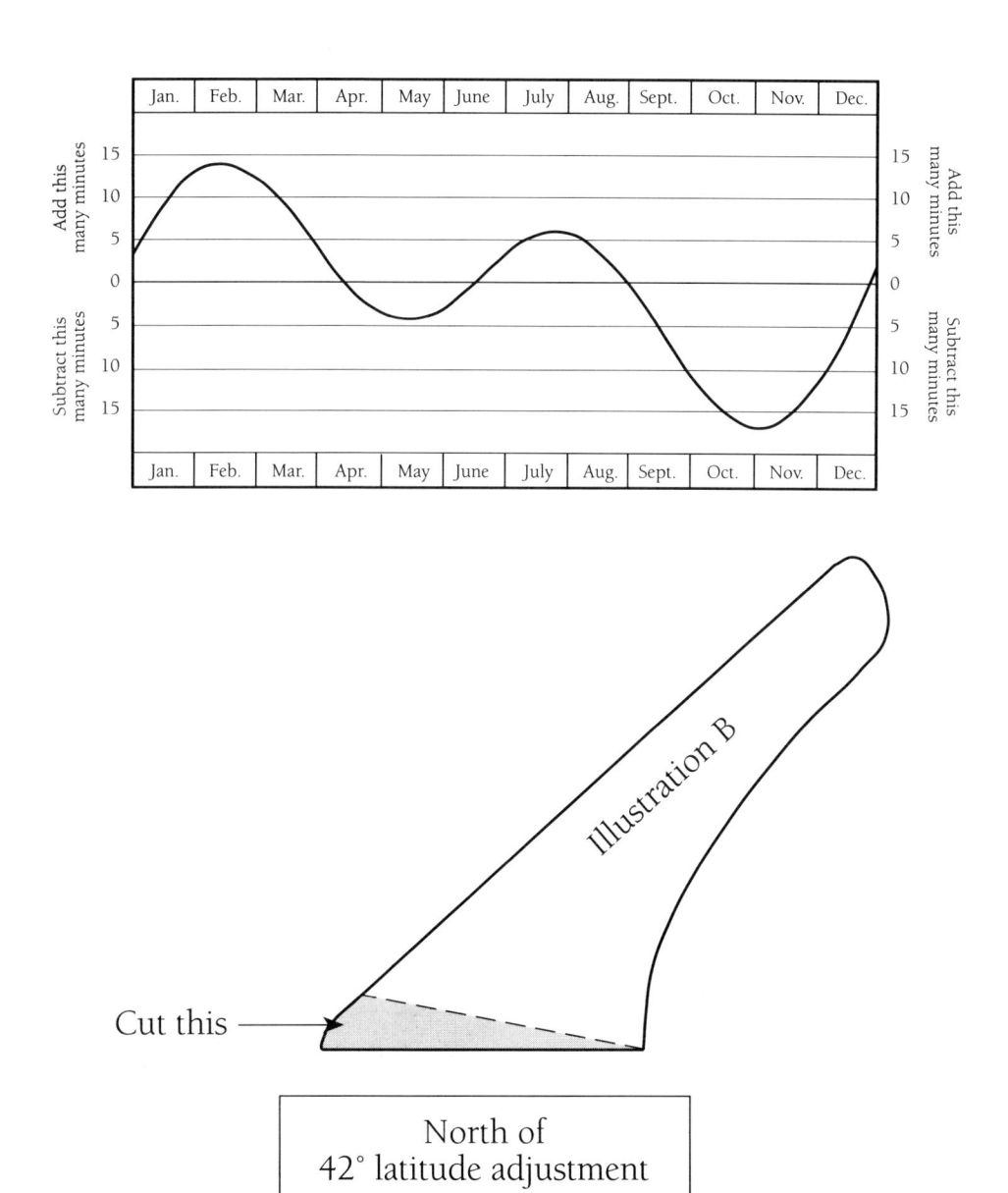

North of
42° latitude adjustment

PART THREE:
LIVING IN ROME IN 10 B.C.

The Second Hour: At Marcus's House

It was still dark when the day began in ancient Rome. Most people rose before dawn to get a head start on the day's activities. Most mornings a great crowd of people gathered at the door of Marcus's house to greet his father. Marcus's father was a very powerful senator. Two years before he had served as consul, the highest office in the state, along with Augustus himself. Before that he had been one of Augustus's most trusted generals. Many people depended on the senator for all kinds of help: legal help, loans of money, and even baskets of food, which the servants handed out every morning to the people who came to call.

The senator would spend the first hour of almost every day with the people who came to greet him. Marcus spent part of this time standing beside his father's chair, listening as his father talked to his clients. The senator looked

PART THREE: LIVING IN ROME IN 10 B.C.

very impressive. His toga was draped beautifully about him, and its purple border stood out against the finely woven, creamy white wool.

The clients gathered before the great chair in which Marcus's father sat. So many today! Beside the chair stood a special servant whose job was to remember the names of the clients. The senator knew most of them, but he often asked the servant, just to be sure. The man speaking to the senator now was wearing a soiled toga and looked very worried. Perhaps he was being called into court and needed Marcus's father to act as his lawyer. Marcus's father was one of the best speakers in Rome. He seldom spoke on behalf of private citizens unless an important question of state was involved. Nevertheless, few people went from this door disappointed: the senator would surely promise his help, and would get one of his younger friends to represent this client. The man began to look relieved, and even to smile a bit. He kissed the senator's hand, bowed down low, and went away.

Many of the clients seemed well-dressed and cheerful, and did not press forward to petition the

49

senator. Then Marcus realized why: they were not here to ask favors, but to repay them. They would be escorting his father down to the Campus Martius after the morning greeting was over. The thought of the entrance his father would make caused Marcus to feel proud. Someday he would sit in the atrium of his own house greeting clients himself, and would allow them to escort him to the courts, to the senate house, and to the imperial palace. And he would know just how to act: he learned a lot by just watching and listening to his father.

Most days Marcus went off to school before the second hour with Agathon, his tutor. Today was different, though. Elsewhere in the city, in the open spaces of the Campus Martius, a huge crowd was gathering to witness the dedication of the great sundial that had been built there

Part Three: Living in Rome in 10 b.c.

in honor of Augustus. The ceremony would take place later, and Marcus's father would attend, of course. There was no need for senators to arrive early to find good places to stand; special seats were reserved for them because of their importance.

After the ceremony, Marcus's father would hurry home as fast as he could, because today was also a family holiday. It was the naming day of a new baby born into the family of Philip, a freedman of Marcus's father. At the ninth hour, there would be a party in honor of the new baby, and the family would be on holiday. For Marcus this meant no school, and a chance to watch the preparations that were underway.

The Third Hour: At Charite's House

Charite tried to spend this morning as she spent every morning, working at her loom. Her mother had taught her how to spin, and would soon begin teaching her to weave as well. Both were good crafts to know in case Charite had to earn money when she grew up, and besides, they were the traditional tasks of all Roman women. Her mother encouraged Charite to do all the Roman things: to dress in the Roman style and to pronounce her Latin carefully and properly, just like the daughter of a senator or a knight. Charite was very good at this, and the reading and writing lessons she took in the afternoons helped a lot. But no matter how good she was at doing Roman things, she loved the lullabies that her mother had sung to her in Greek when she was small, and sometimes she sang them to herself.

Charite's home was in a different region from that of Marcus's house. It was not so grand, either, though it was comfortable. Charite's family lived in an apartment building, or *insula*, which was owned by Marcus's mother. They had not always lived here. Before Charite was born, her father, Philip, and her mother, Lyde, were slaves in Marcus's house. Philip's family had once been free Greeks, but then had lived as slaves in Marcus's household for generations. Lyde's parents became slaves during a war, and Marcus's mother purchased her because she was good at spinning and weaving wool. Marcus's mother thought they would be a good match and encouraged them to be married.

Marcus's family had many slaves, but Philip had been one of the most important. He was assistant to the *dispensator* [dis-pen-SAH-tore], who was in charge of the entire household. In this position, Philip had learned a lot about doing business in Rome: bookkeeping, where to buy things at a good price; and how to manage a large staff. He also learned what the great families in Rome were like: how they lived, what their tastes were in food, clothing,

PART THREE: LIVING IN ROME IN 10 B.C.

furniture, and such, and what sort of people they liked to do business with. Philip was very good at his job, and became a great favorite of Marcus's mother. He was also ambitious, and after a few years had saved up enough money to buy his own and Lyde's freedom. When he told Marcus's mother of his plans, she conferred with the senator and persuaded him to make Philip and Lyde a gift of their freedom and to help set them up in a business of their own.

Charite was just a baby at that time. She didn't remember living in the senator's house. She was excited because today the senator's whole family would be visiting. She had never met them before, so she was looking forward to that, and she knew there was a boy in the family just about her age. She was a little nervous that she wouldn't know how to act in front of such aristocratic visitors, but her mother had told her not to worry and just be herself.

By coming today, Marcus's family was simply fulfilling their obligation to their liberated freedmen, who were celebrating an addition to their family: Charite's baby brother, Lucius!

Activity: Make a Roman Meal

The main meal in the typical Roman day took place in the late afternoon. The dining room of a Roman house was called a *triclinium* [tree-KLIN-ee-oom) because it held three (*tri-*, as in "tricycle") couches on which to lie down. Three people could sit on each couch. Different courses were brought in to the diners on small tables.

PART THREE: LIVING IN ROME IN 10 B.C.

Even though the Romans lived hundreds of years ago, you can still eat the types of food they ate. Here are a few of their favorites that you can make too!
* Drinks: All Romans, including children, would drink wine throughout the meal. You can imitate them by drinking grape juice.
* Appetizers: Fresh sticks of celery and carrots were as popular then as they are today. Olives or hard-boiled eggs were other favorites.
* Main dishes: Veal and chicken were two popular Roman dishes. These were often served fried, along with boiled or fresh vegetables.
* Desserts: Serve an assortment of fresh and dried fruit and nuts, seasoned with honey and sprinkled with spices.

The Fourth Hour: Philip at Work

Philip was listening to ten people at once. They were speaking at least three different languages, and they were all shouting. But Philip was calm. One of the reasons he had done so well for himself was that he could think clearly in situations like this. And a good thing, too! Every important family in Rome was having a party today, and it seemed that they all needed something from him—tents, live animals imported from overseas, musicians, extra servants, and every kind of food and drink. Whenever important people like Marcus's parents needed something special for a gift or to decorate their homes—bouquets of fresh flowers, for example—or needed help with something difficult, like moving a heavy but delicate object, such as a statue, they turned to Philip. He always managed to solve the problem with ease. Having such a good reputation meant that every day he was busy. But today was one of his busiest days ever. He would be glad when the eighth hour had arrived and he could go home to Lucius's party.

After settling things with his customers, Philip turned to speak with his assistant. "Can you handle the rest, Lygdamus?" he asked.

"I think so, Philip, so long as you have taken care of the snow. That is what everyone seems to want," Lygdamus replied.

Philip laughed. Sweat was streaming down Lygdamus's face, which was as red as a beet. "Small wonder, in this heat! You look like a boiled lobster, old friend! Better have a cool drink youself, before you melt!"

Part Three: Living in Rome in 10 b.c.

It *was* hot. The month Sextilis was always hot, but this year was worse than usual. It used to be that the city would empty out a bit as people who could afford to went to the shore or to the mountains where it was cooler. Lately, though, more people had been staying for the official celebration of the emperor Augustus's birthday, which had become bigger each year. More people in the city meant that everyone needed all the usual things from Philip, but that was no problem, and it meant more business. The problem was that it was so hot, and everyone wanted to serve cold drinks. But this late in the summer, snow was in very short supply.

"Thank you, Philip! I will have that drink—although think what I could sell it for; the demand is so great!"

Philip chuckled. Lygdamus was a shrewd businessman. Philip hoped, one day, to set Lygdamus up on his own, but not until little Lucius had grown up and learned the business for himself. "You may sell whatever is here at the going rate. But don't even mention the supply in the other warehouse! I need it for my own party, and in this heat we will be lucky to get it home before it melts!"

The Eighth Hour: Lucius's Naming Party

Charite had never seen so many people in her apartment. For a while she was very shy. She didn't know most of them, and her parents were so busy that they couldn't pay much attention to her. But something happened to cheer her up. All of a sudden, the room got very quiet. How could so many people be so quiet? It was time for the ceremony, when her father would announce the new baby's name to all the guests, and everyone listened carefully.

Philip took the baby, showed him to the guests and announced, "Ladies and gentlemen: I give you my son, Lucius Cornelius Philippus!"

Everyone clapped their hands and came up to congratulate the family. Charite was feeling happy for her family when a boy her age came up to her. From the way he was dressed, she could tell who he was.

"Are you Marcus?" she asked eagerly.

"Yes!" he said.

Marcus smiled at her. "You must be Charite. My mother told me your whole family was clever. Do you go to school? I am starting to learn Greek!"

Hearing this, Charite answered him in Greek. "Of course

PART THREE: LIVING IN ROME IN 10 B.C.

I go to school! Not today, because of the party, but usually I have lessons in Latin, arithmetic—"

"Wait, not so fast!" Marcus laughed. "I said I was just beginning. How do you know so much?"

Charite apologized, saying that her mother often spoke Greek to her at home, and repeated her answer in Latin.

"Oh," said Marcus, "I didn't have lessons today, either. My father took me down to the Campus Martius for the opening of a new monument. It's amazing! A sundial as big as the Forum almost, with a pointer from Egypt, and Augustus's birthday. . . Father explained it, but it's hard to remember it all. He says he'll take me back one day when it's less crowded." Then he got an idea. "Would you like to come?"

Before Charite could answer the nurse interrupted. "Charite!" she said. "Someone important is wanting to meet you. Come quickly!"

Charite rose and scurried after the nurse, with Marcus close behind. They made their way to the front of the room where her father was standing, still holding the baby and beaming with pride. A tall man was with him, looking like a much larger version of Marcus.

"Ah!" said the man, "Here is the young lady I want to meet! I see you already know my son." He smiled in Marcus's direction.

"Father," said Marcus eagerly, "can Charite come when we go back to visit the sundial again? I told her all about it. Please?"

"Of course, son," answered the senator. "You and I

might just need this clever young lady to explain to us how the thing works! An amazing design, Philip," said the senator, turning to Charite's father. "Really clever. You'd be fascinated."

At that moment a waiter appeared with a tray of cool drinks. Philip handed one to the senator and to each of the children, then took one for himself.

"By Jupiter!" exclaimed the senator. "This is the fifth party I've attended this month and the first cold drink I've had at any of them. Well, done, Philip!"

"At your service, sir!" replied Charite's father, bowing low. "After all, this party is in honor of your namesake. It was the least I could do!"

PART FOUR:
THE ROMANS AND THEIR INFLUENCE TODAY

How Their Legacy Influences Our Lives

People often speak about "the fall of the Roman Empire," but it would be hard to say when this actually happened. Even under some of the greatest emperors, like Diocletian, Constantine, and Justinian, the empire was very different from what it had been under Augustus or Trajan. As late as 800 A.D. the French king Charlemagne was crowned Emperor of Rome, and for centuries more there existed something called the Holy Roman Empire. From the very beginning, Rome and its empire were always changing, and their influence continues today.

The city of Rome today is quite different from what it was 2,000 years ago, but traces of the old city remain. The part of the city that remains most as it was is the Forum. There you can see the ruins of many monumental buildings: temples, the senate house, arches built in honor of great military victories, and, at the south end of the Forum, the Colosseum. Archeologists have been working in this area to learn more about how the ancient Romans lived.

In other areas of the city you can see parts of old buildings that have been reused in newer buildings. At the north end of the Forum is the Capitoline Hill. On the other side of the hill is the Theater of Marcellus, a building similar to the Colosseum. Years after it was built, part of the theater collapsed. Later, the parts that remained were used in a new building. At first you might pass this building without noticing the theater, but if you look closely, you can easily tell which are the older and which the newer parts.

There are even some places in Rome where the old buildings have disappeared but have left traces that we can still see. In the Campus Martius, some parts of Augustus's sundial can still be seen: his tomb, the Altar of Peace (which has been moved from its original position), and the obelisk (which has also been moved to the plaza in front of the Palazzo Montecitorio). One of the best-preserved ancient buildings in Rome is the Pantheon, which is near the center of the Campus Martius. Also in the Campus there is a large open plaza, very long and narrow, called the Piazza Navona, which is usually full of people sitting in the cafes that surround it and on the sides of the fountains in the middle of the plaza. The Piazza Navona used to be a circus, or race track, built by the emperor Domitian [doe-MISH-un]. Chariot races, which the Romans loved, used to take place here on special occasions. It is easy to stand in the center of the piazza and imagine the sound of the horses' hooves and the noise of the crowd rooting for their favorite teams.

The Romans built cities throughout their empire, which extended from the border between Scotland and England in the north, down through western Germany to Rumania and south to Greece and Turkey, the Middle East, the Arabian peninsula, and across northern Africa all the way to Spain

PART FOUR: THE ROMANS AND THEIR INFLUENCE TODAY

and Portugal in the west. Throughout this area there are remains of towns, buildings, roads, and monuments built by the Romans. The Italian, Spanish, French, Portugese, and Rumanian languages, along with several others, are modern versions of the Latin that was spoken in these areas when they were Roman provinces.

But we don't have to travel far to find traces of the Romans. Many of our words come from Latin words: the United States Senate is named after and partly modeled on the Roman senate, and our Capitol building is named after the Roman Capitolium—the Capitoline Hill, where the main temple of Jupiter was. Our Capitol building, together with many other pieces of public architecture, imitate Roman building styles. One of our most important building materials is concrete, and this, too, was a Roman invention. Almost everywhere we look we can find traces of the Romans, and the more we get to know them, the more we understand about ourselves.

One of the many buildings influenced by Roman architecture, the U.S. Capitol

ABOUT THE AUTHOR

Dr. Joseph Farrell is Associate Professor of Classical Studies at the University of Pennsylvania, where he teaches Latin language and literature and Roman culture. Dr. Farrell has written and edited several books and articles on classical subjects. He lives in Philadelphia with his wife, Ann de Forest, their daughter, Flannery, who is six, and their son, Kai, who is two.